A Child's Day
Heidi's Way

Written and Illustrated by Nancy L. Bentley

Copyright © 2015 Nancy L Bentley

Written and Illustrated by Nancy L. Bentley

All rights reserved.

ISBN:0692603816
ISBN-13:9780692603819

DEDICATION

To my children and grandchildren who inspire me and bring me such joy. Because of them I have learned a lot of life lessons that can't be learned any other way! Thanks to Richard my husband and my two youngest boys, Bryson and Branton, for helping with all the details in making this book.

Have you ever had a day that you wish would go away? Now I'm not trying to say that it always happens that way.

Most days are good; you would be impressed, really you would.

The day started out boring and then it started soaring. Everything just happened fast.

One thing after another; first yelling at my sister…

…. then fighting with my brother, then hiding from my mother. Boy what a day, what can I say, I felt like running away!

I was hiding in the coat closet, when my nose ran a stream...

I tried to be quiet and freeze, my nose ran like a faucet......

... so I let out a sneeze.

The door opened quickly, I saw two shoes. They were red, I hid my head. It was my mother;

I thought she was mad....so I became sad. Boy I thought I was had!

...I burst into tears because of my fears, and then I couldn't believe my ears.

She said, "I love you, my dear." She wiped away my tears and picked me up and held me tight. She said, "Please don't fight. I love all of you kids."

I felt bad for the problems I had caused. … So I said I was sorry to my mother and to my sister and to my brother. I really felt sorry for fighting.

They smiled and hugged me, my day got better as you can see.

Mom gathered us around her to read….

…....then up to the table to eat.

**Then off for a nap, snug in our beds,
we rested our heads.**

Later, after our naps ... we three
went out to play and had a good
time the rest of the day.......

...we climbed trees and gathered leaves.

Rode our bikes, we played all day long.

Later into the house for dinner with
Mom and Dad. The food was good
and made us glad.

Stacked the dishes, we all helped out...the chores went quick without a doubt.

With dishes done and the kitchen clean, dad played and talked with each of us... no one made a fuss.

Bedtime came, so we brushed our teeth and said good night.

I said my prayers and went to bed!

It turned out to be a great day. What more can I say... oh yeah good night!

THE END!

4

www.ingramcontent.com/pod-product-compliance
Lightning Source LLC
Chambersburg PA
CBHW041745040426
42444CB00001B/39